UGLY DUCKLING PRESSE :: DOSSIER

Ten Walks/Two Talks
Copyright © 2010 by Jon Cotner and Andy Fitch

ISBN: 978-1-933254-67-8

Thanks to the Donald D. Walker Collection, Prints & Photographs Division, Library of Congress, for making available high-quality digital images of the following prints by Hiroshige: *Nihonbashi yukibare, Yotsuya naitō shijuku, Toranomon-soto aoizaka, Ōji fudō no taki*

The epigraph comes from Cid Corman's *Back Roads to Far Towns: Bashō's Travel Journal*. Used with permission by White Pine Press, www.whitepine.org.

First Edition 2010
Printed in the USA
Design & typesetting: Macabea Can Type

Ugly Duckling Presse
The Old American Can Factory
232 Third Street #E-002
Brooklyn, NY 11215

This title is part of UDP's Dossier Series, which publishes works in the investigative mode, regardless of genre or format.

For more information about UDP and the Dossier Series, visit us on the Web: www.uglyducklingpresse.org

TEN WALKS/TWO TALKS

Jon Cotner and Andy Fitch

TABLE OF CONTENTS

So—when was it—I, drawn like blown cloud, couldn't stop dreaming of roaming, roving the coast up and down, back at the hut last fall by the riverside, sweeping cobwebs off, a year gone and misty skies of spring returning, yearning to go over the Shirikawa Barrier.

—Bashō

EARLY SPRING

…then broke ranks as they passed smeared horse poop clumps.

MONDAY

Still spinning out Kristin's door I decided to change plans. The air stirred gently, made me think of flags. At 9:26 I saw the clean white backs of waitresses in a Gee Whiz Diner window.

Someone in charcoal suit and tie sprinted across Chambers towards a pharmacy. It hadn't opened. He turned back to his car. I took off my coat and bunched it. I crossed between busses, blinking when a photo of fast-food chicken got in my face, cutting east with a blind woman and her father. A kid weaving a handcart through everyone wore a baseball hat that said C*aire*ful.

Tribeca smelled like soft rolls and coffee. Office towers from the seventies stood tinted pleasant green. All the scaffolds dripped on Broadway. Squares had been torn to let a sapling through. A bush on Franklin held a plump melodic sparrow. A woman smiling at someone behind me waved in case I'd misunderstood. I turned up White but can't remember it. I don't remember Church except for the clapping sound of pigeons' wings. At Canal I dropped into the art-deco post office thinking Union Station L.A. I asked a clerk where to find passport applications.

Monday no passport she said, never looking up. Tuesday Saturday Window 20. Monday Window 20 closed.

Near the exit I passed Window 20. To me it appeared open. From Thompson I remembered dreaming about fire escapes last night. I felt at ease across from six-story columns identified as Shaftways. A parking attendant dragged his chair into the center of the sun. He closed his eyes but kept talking to the co-worker behind him.

A street-sweeping truck followed me down Spring. This scared a floppy spaniel which nonetheless kept up its owner's brisk pace. Two blonds seemed thrilled to be tall and heading to work and more generally everyone looked buoyant. The joy hinted that it would last. Handsome black men took off helmets, walked motor scooters along the curb. My big toe ached from pushing too hard. I stuffed my hat in a coat pocket.

Damp air blowing in from Chinatown smelled like mushroom bulk bins. There were so many 50-pound bags of onions. There were ashy carrots as thick as forearms. I couldn't pause to examine fish but I did appreciate bubbling tanks. I split through murmuring couples. Hunched women stopped to consider produce. Others turned so gradually I saw it coming a hundred feet off. Someone Haitian called out Cel-e-*ry* to his grinning Chinese counterpart: an old guy in appealing thin pants. Behind them somebody mentally retarded passed by unattended, wiggled her foot—pushed beyond the disjointed blocks between Bayard and Confucius Plaza.

One Asian girl in gold tights and sneakers helped an ancient couple cross Catherine. Upon close inspection all three looked gray.

I got to Chatham Square Library just as it opened. The clerk fixated on a tower of DVD check-ins before retrieving my John Cage audio hold. The neighborhood grew steamy. Someone catching crates of strawberries couldn't help squishing each box he caught. Somebody paced herself to pass between boxes. A woman sidled up to a police officer and asked without eye-contact Where's the World Trade?

As we waited out the light one mom started blinking. Her non-glossy freckled skin reminded me of cookies. Soon we were smiling, mostly staring straight ahead. Saturated with goodwill I strode right toward my favorite Bellbates cashier before even grabbing a handcart.

Back at Church a girl's wheelchair glistened. A cook drenched the sidewalk with soapy water. In Park Dayschool it was story time. The woman had gray dreadlocks.

TUESDAY

No one had an umbrella so I assumed it wasn't raining. But from the door I saw drops slap a white garbage bag. By 7:30 pools gathered in its creases.

With snow gone I wanted to check out The Conservatory Gardens. Ducks paddled stoically across The Meer. Swans didn't look distinct yet. Seagulls' feet get so much yellower here than Battery Park. Three women hoisting umbrellas came towards me in a solid line, taking up the entire walk, then broke ranks as they passed smeared horse poop clumps. A wide green garbage truck passed next—I had to spin sideways to let it fit. There was something Japanese about the wobbly boots park workers wore as they speared paper scraps in the rain. The chords geese behind us honked tingled like seltzer.

Chains circled The Gardens. I'd come too early. Plants seemed somehow put away. Where I crossed Fifth a cab almost crushed a girl. She stayed quiet about it. I screamed Idiot through the passenger's window. Through a basement window on E. 102nd I watched great quantities of sandwiches and some mayonnaise-soaked side dish get wrapped. Loosely chopped lettuce heads spilled down a long counter/cutting board. Tins of sliced tomatoes stood red and filled with seeds.

Black school children waited for busses: too many to fit under the fiberglass. At the crowd's edge a blond stroked his tense son's bangs. Are you sure you're ok? he said. You look silly.

Coming out from Long Island Railroad tracks I found a bed-table wallpapered blue with white stars. I turned amid cops in orange rainproof headdress (a straggler jogged behind, chubby and really bending his knees).

On the walk up Lexington it became clear that pedestrians with no umbrellas moved non-committally while people under cover set a quick pace. Between Kim's Nails and Our Laundry sprawling, frustrated groups waited for several busses. A Poland Springs water bottle sailed down the curb. Tough guys clasped hands without ever speaking. One crowded store sold cakes and balloons. A mural for Popate (1973-1994) included a cross-eyed man's portrait, a Puerto Rican flag, a moonlit inscription: From Family And Friends.

As I continued north a contact lens began to flutter. I kept having to stare to dissipate the film. People weren't comfortable with this but the alternate option was to wink a lot. I knew I'd been approaching the Triborough Bridge yet couldn't remember how it connects to the Bronx. Geographically I'd grown confused; it felt like someone might jump me. At 131st, where Lexington ends, a giant Sanitation warehouse starts. Oldies songs drift at modest volumes. Hot twin clerks in an office supply store called out from distant display-room desks.

On the way down Madison my knees began to fade. The evening before I'd biked Manhattan twice. Passing the Mt. Morris Turkish Baths (underground at the corner like any innocuous subway stop) I wondered if they could still possibly exist. The gate blew open, actually. A girl protected by a vinyl rain cap frowned just beyond her mother's umbrella.

Sloshing across Marcus Garvey Park I pushed up stairs with waning strides. At the peak a timid white person approached asking me to sell him a cigarette. Temporarily stunned, I said No thanks. The spiraling tower at the park's tip stood locked. Still there was a pleasing amount of space. The swimming pool lay filled with muck. Through branches Fifth Avenue resembled strips of stars.

The park path dropped me south, which seemed fine, though I'd grown self-conscious about the broken zipper on the khakis I always wear in the rain. A muscular guy's miniature collie yapped at cars but always managed to heel. On 116th a Harlem Sports Club's Coming Soon window-display looked pretty disorganized. On 112th a co-op's multiple doormen suggested high-security gentrification was already well in progress.

On 111th city workers strained to unhook a manhole cover. I'd always wondered if these are heavy. When I paid for orange juice at the nearest bodega a kid asked Y'all got headphones? This stayed inscrutable as I passed through the lobby provisioned and spent.

WEDNESDAY

Kristin came from the elevator, which smelled like coffee. The florists had installed yellow daisies, yellow lilies. At 8:12 I flinched against a frigid gust—couldn't get my lips wedged under a scarf. People's eyes expressed abandonment. I cancelled my walk along the Hudson and scurried toward the island's center. A suitcase held down someone's burrito-wrapped blanket. In the next alcove somebody Hispanic read tabloids atop a milk crate.

Judging from body language boys with facemasks were the coldest. For a block it turned too bright to look past sidewalk. A young malamute lay calmly breathing. Ethereal X's ran up a building façade (these seemed to maybe come from hubcaps). Broadway had been so heavily salted I couldn't gauge how much snow there was. Under Leonard Street scaffolds ice-dust glimmered. A white man slipped then ended up doing the splits near City Hall. A Korean couple in high-tech winter gear spoke intimately, moved gracefully. A bareheaded cop guarding the state courthouse smiled; he appeared to have just remembered something.

Columbus Park had been eviscerated. Pipes lay everywhere. Trucks' blond shovels stood filled with snow. Along a hastily assembled fence I slipped and strained my neck catching balance. Along Baxter Chinese women talked and did aerobics. One's hips wouldn't stop shimmying. I spun off in vicarious ecstasy.

I couldn't feel the cold as a young Asian woman crossed Canal in clogs and yellow neon socks. Behind her men pushed delivery carts: four Andyboy lettuce boxes, four marked TROUT. There weren't any Italians yet on Mulberry. They must all drive in from out of state. One dark-skinned boy chipped away at ice. One door sat surrounded by olive oil tins. The one gay pride flag for blocks had gotten entangled in fire escape steps. Neatly stacked Malaysian newspapers had been bound and stamped Recycling.

Pigeons spread up sidewalk on Grand, tearing at cinnamon-raisin bagels. I plowed through then felt bad approaching their patron—a compact lady with bags. One mom strained to tie garbage bags without taking off gloves. One squat guy hauled heavy cement-mix bags to a pick-up. Each time he spun back to the vestibule he faced chic tall mannequins in short denim skirts. He seemed to appreciate this.

A woman knelt wrapped in verdant shades I'd never seen anybody wear. After we glanced in each other's eyes I looked at flower barrels, a parking garage. Mulberry ended at Lafayette, where someone had written across a bus-stop sign Except there is no such bus on weekends! I walked over subway grates since these felt the least icy. I love any enfolding path of gridded metal squares. I got excited watching a restaurant's cellar door rise. It turned out to be a mechanized process.

Cancun Lounge (adjacent to Woo Lae Oak, my first job in New York) had been converted into a fish-bar with an abstract one-word title. The big design change was slightly more neutral tones. A drop of water fell in my mouth as I passed the store for kid geniuses. A resident's recycling bin overflowed with green bottles. Hispanic contractors huddled in lobbies: except one woman washed windows in just a teal sweatshirt. Someone carrying a load of bricks spaced out, screamed Sorry, crashed into me. Crossing Canal I could barely ignore movie billboards where the tunnel dropped. I straightened as an attractive waitress passed and our faces seemed bizarrely close.

I got confused at the diagonal intersection with Varick and ended up sprinting across in a panic though it turned out I had a walk sign. Tree-branch shadows flickered off busses. Otherwise they didn't exist. A potted fir tipped in front of the French restaurant on Duane. A couple windows hung open in the Cosmopolitan Hotel. Those rooms must have been unbearably hot. On my way back to the elevator, as I passed Raphael, "Hello" never got through my rigid jaws—my lips just moved silently.

THURSDAY

Luis was talking with an older resident when I stepped out of the stairwell. I knew he wanted to remind me of the exterminators coming. I slid brusquely through the arch their bodies made. At 8:17 cold air lay still.

I crossed through scaffolds strung with caged lamps. Icicles and nails poked down near the exit. Silence and light gathered around tabloid salesmen seated on milk crates at 110th and Lenox. Slashed garbage bags spilled their contents. Shredded documents clung to each other. Books sprawled, some flapping. The guy ahead grabbed several without slowing down. There was a Benito Cellini, P.G. Wodehouse, Kathy Acker. There were also hundreds of greeting cards.

Curled shoots like thin green tongues kept unbinding themselves in sidewalk plots. I crouched to read a plant's identification tag. Dark ice showed where bus passengers spilled coffee. Across the street joggers expelled mist onto shrubs—a different morning.

A girl chipped ice off an SUV. She used something small like a credit card, looked 80% hypnotized. A Vermont Bus Lines coach turned south though its destination board read Bangor. An old Jamaican dropped his walkman: scattering silver plastic. He flinched then spun around before stooping to pick things up. After carrying home too many books last night I could barely peek in the farmers' market. My neck and back muscles wouldn't bend. Spasms flickered like lightning bolts somewhere around my kidneys. A dwarf carried her mesh Speedo bag off one shoulder (two bananas inside).

An elderly pedestrian adjusted a yarmulke. His torso stayed bent perpendicular to his legs. The steepest part of this stretch stood covered in paper cups and pieces of rolls from subway platforms. People are always tossing out rolls. Staring at a departed 9-train felt like almost remembering something. Boy Scouts distributed carwash flyers. At 125th I turned east.

A blonde Hispanic woman cradled a child wrapped in pastel blankets—even its face. Amid blue sky and snow someone winding down the path from a General Grant Housing Project caught my attention. He looked at home here. The restrictive internal cramps I used to get around housing projects were gone. This happened across from a place called El Tina. A man murmured Cigarettes. Cigarettes. Cigarettes.

A crumbling marquee read Welcome to Harlem, U.S.A. At the corner someone slowed, muttered Marlboros, Newports. Copy machines rusted under traffic lights. Vendors laid blankets on plywood tables. The crossing guard beside me blew her whistle. My thighs began chafing against my jeans.

(Just as expected) it became hard to walk one of Manhattan's main east-west thoroughfares without mostly losing consciousness. One girl's backpack was a yarn head with dreadlocks.

Cutting through Marcus Garvey Park I recognized the hysterical collie from Tuesday's walk. The dog sprinted in diminishing circles. Its master kept handing himself the leash overhead. Snow caught in masonite reminded me of etchings. A pit bull wore an expensive red top. Pale boys shied along the fence and stared at the owner. She seemed happy with that.

Back on my own block I studied birdhouses nestled within a gingko. A bulbous sparrow peeked out from one. A businesswoman ate a big doughnut for breakfast. I ended up liking today.

FRIDAY

I spun out from Kristin's at 8:14 against the enlivening gravelly air. Business people passed by harried and alone. Cement trucks corkscrewed past. Across Greenwich a woman exiting a cab clenched her butt. She was into herself and wore all white.

Around Harrison dusty workers smoked beneath a giant blue Putzmeister crane. Why do fenced-off construction sites make me feel small, lonely and connected to the world? Skyscrapers along the New Jersey coast all looked the same color as my personal checks. One storefront rivaled Milton's description of Chaos. Placards put Jesus in blindfold next to a blind, grinning Mao. Only after a cart filled with recyclables had passed did I realize how oblivious I'd been of its presence. Pomeranians slowed to stare at poodles across the street.

Crowds converged on Citicorp's building as if by gravitational pull. A boy squatting with a laptop smiled (which completely hid his lips). Crossing Canal, listening to a couple murmur inside one car, it felt like I was still sleeping. Ahead of me an architect explained that what people call her quirky designs are just attempts to avoid all this lifelessness. Somebody blind scanned the intersection with his cane. Fingers peeked from a homeless person's quilt. Behind this someone else lay covered. The fresh morning smell had changed to damp boots.

I gazed into the dusty stillness of a sedan's rear dashboard and then there was a bible there. I passed a UPS warehouse in which you could just make out the workers' breaths. West African security guards joked with shippers, who stayed slightly more serious. Nothing rode on the conveyor belts. All of this repeated itself for blocks: 136 parking spaces. Afterwards Fed Ex began which somehow seemed less interesting.

From Perry a jogger passed in shorts and I remembered I'd soon see a lot of flesh in public. Kids grouped around a crossing guard might have all been models. Preoccupied women strode past in leather pants. Two bags of piss leaned against a tree. Two rotund men in shades wore their blue and white headdress like Yasser Arafat's. Everybody else paused walking a dog. A basset pup wouldn't sniff a magnolia, no matter how aggressive its owner's commands.

Crossing Jane I looked just as a mother yawned; I felt a part of this. A dad and son drank blue Elixir concoctions through straws. Amid bobbing tulips I saw that Congress opened Alaska for 24 billion barrels of oil. At Taylor's Bakery blonde women sipped chai as their daughters sampled rice-krispie squares.

Shimmering lawns surrounded St. Luke in the Fields, restored my faith in the variety of birds. I got lost remembering songs by The Smiths. A sophisticated old black woman held up a coffee-stand line asking why she'd only been charged a dollar fifty. A prep cook shielded his gold-toothed smile. Construction guys turned to watch a redhead pass. The shortest carried bags of gears on his shoulder. As I crossed he said Except she'd only be wearing ski boots.

In an alcove on Jay a cop and his daughter shared a chocolate doughnut with pink jimmies. A knife knocked chicken cubes along a deli counter. I stepped through scattered proof pages chopped in thirds. My biggest criticism of nurses, one read, is that they often treat the patient to fit the pattern. Your nurse thinks, "I've got four patients to bathe before coffee break." The feeling she communicates is, "You're going to brush your teeth whether you like it or not." I flipped the scrap over: After I returned home from the hospital that winter [1978], I would crawl up stairs on my hands and knees. I was too unsteady to walk.

Without conscious effort I turned west on Duane, avoided the TV mounted at Chambers. Brothers did push-ups along the pavement with someone about sixty smiling above them. An onion stood against a scooter wheel beside the entrance steps to Salaam Bombay. The garbage bins overflowed with nan.

An old man on a treadmill wore headphones, cotton slacks, wingtips. I wondered how it felt to wear one woman's heels. Across from Baluchi's somebody told her boyfriend All this shit happened be*fore* your ass. Everything reflected off nearby windows, where waiters dished out chutneys.

EARLY WINTER

"Tonight seems warm for January."

CENTRAL PARK, 9:10 p.m.

J: What do you think of this New York lavender sky?

A: I've walked through this sky several hours now. I started at 110th Street.

J: You visited your old building?

A: Well I never actually look at it. I pretended I'd lived on the the edge of The Meer—the Meer's of course the pond up there. I don't fully retrace steps. But how wonderful to step off a subway, to climb stairs and hear hockey pucks slam Lasker Rink, formerly Lasker Pool.

J: Right with games going on or kids practicing?

A: Kids practiced, which might sound dissatisfying, yet it delighted me to find black kids practicing. I'd thought only rich white people use that edge of the park: carrying in expensive accessories. Perhaps you've noticed, if you've glanced at the rink, that it's heavily funded by Donald Trump (sorry to mention such a stupid name).

J: I wouldn't…

A: Trump gets printed on everything…

J: That…

A: bouncing off ice like blood. Though the place supports diverse hockey crews.

J: Is this bright restaurant Tavern on the Green?

A: Yes it is. Look there.

J: Haven't you attended parties here with...

A: I have; I do...

J: Kristin?

A: miss them, strangely, standing with my love and her kind boss and co-workers. Nobody thinks the food's good. But we'd end up on patios...

J: Oh yeah?

A: with silverware clinking.

J: Sure I'd wanted to cross the park today, but spent hours printing a writing sample for UCSD: a total, maddening loss of time. In fact one guy caught me losing my cool. I explained only printer troubles...

A: Let's move down the mic a bit.

J: make me lose my cool.

A: I got I got caught bowing to the Huddlestone Arch waterfall by this shadowy figure who...

J: A scary...

A: squinted, and seemed to want me not to say anything. I passed on. I scurried away.

J: You once claimed for years, upon waking, you'd bow to your bed. Was that true?

A: True but since I've stopped. I'd bow as I approached the bed and woke up. Or in Boston I'd say Goodbye instead of Good night to our friends David and Stephen, thinking Death may separate us before these eyes re-open.

J: So in bowing you bent and acknowledged…you wished to welcome new mornings?

A: Yes, and also the fact a third of life takes place not as a conscious autonomous being. I'd…

J: Right.

A: organize the rest, what what I call "my" days…I'll organize remaining time around this, as though it weren't there. By bowing I could mark the void of that experience, at least…

J: Since you tracked it.

A: trace its shores. Still I stopped because I got embarrassed around Kristin. Bowing's something you shouldn't feel embarrassed by, yet for that reason hard to explain. For a year I'd move my eyes up and down—the way people check out a person, but at the bed. Gradually that felt silly too.

J: Well if you think about it: the bed recharges you. It's also the place you hold your...

A: True, though we sleep far apart and prefer separate blankets. I make minute adjustments all night that...

J: Really.

A: infuriate everybody.

J: When we split a room in Somerville, you slept with socks pulled down past your heels for ventilation.

A: Yeah, the my slippers I like to call those. Um you mentioned yesterday, I believe yesterday, the need for climate control with these talks. In the past I've strode through frigid temperatures thinking As a native of the Midwest I encountered far...

J: Through froz...

A: [*Muffled*] scornful of people cringing or with red-tipped ears.

J: I remember how how cold I'd felt last winter in Milwaukee.

A: But ever since I started caring about language, I've become someone who tries to transport his environment, to stay in the most lucid state. Do you feel similar or will you whip off your scarf and flaunt it?

J: Oh I make adjustments all the time. That's why I've carried this backpack. I had no idea I'd use a second sweater today, yet when I learned we'd cross through Central Park, took it out immediately. Also this past summer, doing work in Santa Fe, I'd adjust the fan so it couldn't blow directly on me, but a few minutes later I'd shift the fan back toward me, to cool off.

A: This was while attempting to sleep?

J: No this is studying. I think I've...well I know I strained to understand Ptolemy's astronomy, and if required to read his *Almagest* I'd turn warmer, yet could handle fan breeze only so long.

A: Sure. Have you noticed this man going at lampposts with what I'd consider a Thai boxing style—lots of knee, knee, knee-thrusts?

J: It's certainly not jujitsu.

A: Just as...

J: I could imagine he gets invaluable practice. The lampposts allow him to hone some moves.

A: this afternoon I tried (while on the phone with Kristin) spinning like a ballerinA: lifting one foot so that your knee stands, so that your thigh hangs parallel to ground...

J: Right.

A: lifting...or holding a foot perpendicular and twirling? I forgot centripetal force...

J: Did you stretch new muscles?

A: I felt like the vessel of a greater motion.

J: Lots of fences splitting the park and…

A: I'll hate…

J: roped-off yards.

A: I hate to make you see this, yes; The Mall of American Elms, one one of my favorite places, lies fenced and ugly. Of course we could slip that fence behi…

J: Yeah who knows how those trees endured the plague which…

A: Yes. Yes.

J: brought down their brethren.

A: Do cities provide impenetrable islands? Did blights have no path to get here? Or could they travel, let's say, on hikers' soles?

J: Well around the Harvard campus you don't find elms. Once I heard a tour guide make that remark while cutting, as I walked toward the Science Center to use the bathroom. But I'm not sure if Manhattan's elms escaped most plagues or if here stands the tiny pocket which survived.

A: You'd asked about this violet light, which strongly resembles a *One Hundred Famous Views of Edo* print, or *hei*-do as Yuki taught me to say it.

J: Ooh. Putting stress in the right place, yeah?

A: A place I can't describe. A place I could mimic but not define for anyone. The print shows I believe plums blossoming, and plum blossoms don't look this color yet the sky does in the print. Perhaps lavender suggests this time of night. As always in winter months I've I value Asian, specifically Japanese art, for training us to recognize the splendor of bare branches.

J: That's why I go back to Asian poetry and painting, to to track the beauty of each season but not catch myself…and escape the trap of longing for summer in the heart of winter.

A: Right.

J: I mean think about it: if trees hung full we'd be walking under canopies, a canopy of leaves and wouldn't see this violet sky, which seems unique to Manhattan or a major industrial city. I never saw it in St. Louis growing up, or Boston.

A: I'd see it in Wisconsin some nights of fresh snowfall. You'd find reflective qualities similar to this, a refractive luminosity, and I don't know if sky gets generated from…

J: I do sense a…

A: haze? A haze of lamplight diffused…

J: Exactly.

A: diffused somehow? Then reformed as mauve canopy?

J: Think…

A: Hard to explain.

J: that since all fumes…

A: Jon can we try the acoustics in the—what do we call this?

J: An amphitheater.

A: Yes the amphitheater. But now go ahead…

J: Yeah, I feel we've stepped back to 5th century B.C. This amphi-
theater looks archaic.

A: I've never taken those stairs behind it.

J: Nor have I stood on the stage. Circumstances haven't seemed
appropriate. Often you'll pass roller-bladers…we won't be able to
get inside.

A: Oh, we can just climb up.

J: Oh is that right?

A: I thought we could slip through but…and what is this?

J: This looks…

A: A little vineyard?

J: An an arbor. Wow.

A: Do you mind?

J: No not at all. How wonderful.

A: I've wanted, on my walk here I didn't climb Belvedere Castle, which always...

J: Well let's do that.

A: [*Roaring jet*] landscape. Should we do that?

J: Sure. But as I was saying, I'd think damp fumes—just look at this grape vine.

A: The trunk itself could be a gargoyle.

J: It does resemble stone, doesn't it? It seems that sturdy and dense. Perhaps these vines yield fruit. They're hearty.

A: They may. Though I laughed when you made a a somewhat critical reference to roller-bladers, I did see a roller-blader curve earli...

J: Oh we shouldn't...

A: and felt myself curving too.

J: I didn't make a critical reference. I said I've seen some life-bladers, some roller-bladers, risk their lives jumping from stage...

A: Oh right: we'd wanted to cross that stage.

J: down to pavement. Not, I don't think we can. The doorway...

A: We just climb up.

J: I saw a locked door. What did you see? [*Pause*]

A: Sorry to pull hard. But look at the Time Warner Center (where we began) through...

J: Look at that.

A: a net of overlapping branches, different dry-leaf and berry patterns—two towers meant to resemble a drawbridge? Maybe?

J: Um you see a drawbridge; I see batter...a nine-volt battery. If you stare above this dome the sky looks white.

A: Yeah now...

J: Do you see that?

A: Yes. Now that is definitely urban sheen.

J: Blocking out blackness from the heavens?

A: Though the heavens don't look black, right?

J: Well they twinkle with...

A: Yeah, yeah. Illuminating.

J: Do do you remember when we walked Santa Fe's hills bathed in moonlight?

A: I felt naked yet had three layers on.

J: It got so cold, do you remember? And the next afternoon we hiked a mountain behind St. John's but...

A: The sheet of ice...

J: often slipped because of ice, then called it a day.

A: We are going to climb up now. [*Silence*] Now—acoustics stay impressive here, but better at the lip of of the stage.

J: Expertly designed. Our voices do acquire uncharacteristic fullness...

A: Right since...

J: as though we've trained in opera.

A: Or if you wanted to convey distance in a scene: when actors step back they'd sound further away, granted...

J: That's a good point.

A: these varying acoustics.

J: So you think amphitheaters came about through collaboration between actors and architects?

A: I'd I've never understood how amphitheater patterns...here we have what, recessed octagonal...

J: Yeah with rosette decorations. Beautiful.

A: It is, but whenever a hall I visit has praiseworthy acoustics it contains some sort of withdrawn, recessed pattern, like...

J: You could say concave.

A: Concave. A concave pattern, and I can't tell...

J: A concavity.

A: if that amplifies sound, or allows sound to shimmer like the stars you've described.

J: Well if if your voice bounces...if if if we think about voices in the "crude" atomic way Lucretius...

A: Sure. Let's.

J: When speaking we expel atoms, which bounce off these walls at various points but, since the structure turns concave, a greater percentage of reflected atoms reach our ears than if this wall stood perpendicular to...

A: Though is it large quantities reach our ears or that, with the plenitude of angles at which things collide in the moment, you'll find great diffusion and more balanced sound?

J: Lucretius would say a a greater number of atoms reach our individual ears, and that the same applies for each audience member.

A: Shall we continue towards the Polish king?

J: Right let's do that.

A: Jiollo, is that his name? Ji, Ji...

J: I won't, I'm not sure.

A: Jioello? I'd passed him earlier tonight.

J: My mother's never been to New York City, but now that I'll have my own apartment the next few weeks I might surprise her with a plane ticket. She'd love Central Park and since she has Polish blood, a Polish heritage, I thought about this king's statue and how she would enjoy looking at him. In photos my grandfather resembles the Polish king.

A: Have you noticed how much easier it is to to stumble upon the Polish king than to purposely find him?

J: Of course.

A: I've tried to lead us directly toward him.

J: We've proved many mystical doctrines through the example of this Polish king. I remember Asian poems about a nervousness that seizes us as we aim for the target: how the archer in competition can't shoot near a bull's-eye, yet with the stakes low he or she hits right on.

A: That's not a metaphor? Too bad this tunnel's closed. I'll love...

J: Is it closed?

A: Yes and I love the smell in there.

J: Last century's urine?

A: It reeks of millennia. But I—in my trip through the park, on the way here—felt stunned. First I saw a red fire…a save-someone-who-fell-through-broken-ice ladder. I'd guess you know these get affixed to many water, to sites of, bodies of water in the park?

J: Right. So not The Harlem Meer?

A: Some hang there but this was not there. This was in fact The Loch.

J: And just so I know, M-e-e-r…

A: Correct.

J: spells the Dutch word for pond?

A: That makes sense. It makes sense because water reflects. From…

J: Because Harlem's Dutch.

A: They could have built a reflective pond. I mean Olmstead designed this park, with the other person whose name no one remembers, and that happened mid-19th…

J: Hmm.

A: But whether the pond appeared before Olmstead imagined…

J: Which came...

A: Hard to say. I know the bluff got used both in the Revolutionary War and the War of 1812—a strategic site. So with the bluff the bluff...perhaps ponds existed also. Here's a red ladder.

J: You'd started to explain.

A: Spotting ladders triggered my memory and I relived a year ago, my life a year ago, which felt infinitely far...

J: Infinitely: many, many...

A: These acoustics push that time further away, much like on the stage...

J: Previous...

A: we crossed. And I realized how cool life was last year without my intending or noticing at the time, that...

J: A healthy realization.

A: at this hour of night, long winter nights, I'd bike home from class. What a great thing.

J: Hunter, right?

A: A Hunter College professor.

J: Yeah, and the coolest syllabus around. As I remember: Thoreau's *Walden*, James Schuyler's *Morning of the Poem*, and then Claudia Rankine's *Don't Let Me Be Lonely*—which by the way I have. You'd lent your copy and I...

A: Terrific.

J: brought it with me.

A: Thanks. I would, for example, finish one class at four yet start again at eight, and ride the bike between...

J: What a splendid existence.

A: thinking it inconvenient to have such a job, but now I know I'd coast through worlds of beauty.

J: You biked home. You fixed dinner. And then you went back?

A: Yes. Yes. Yes.

J: And would you give the same...

A: Like Wittgenstein I couldn't tolerate verbal corpses and...

J: Exactly.

A: spoke new words later on.

J: Pulling students into the conversation I bet.

A: Not sure. As we pass The Boathouse to...

J: Oh, do you smell the pine?

A: Yeah I do.

J: It's a lovely smell, and those branches looked a lovely pale green. Did you notice?

A: Especially against the golden light.

J: This feels like Scandinavia. [*Silence*]

A: But so on the walk from 110th, as I reflected on seasonal continuity—which became a dominant motif in my head after crossing this park so many...

J: Sure.

A: I felt um, discouraged would be an understatement, by the fact we don't, that we can't rely on seasons any longer, because of global warming. Normally I'm not programmatic, but until global warming gets addressed lyric poets should remain improvers, continually, however exhausting.

J: Meaning we can't settle ourselves amid nature's vocabulary while while this vocabulary disappears along with realities to which it corresponds?

A: Disappearing, suffering huge...

J: I know I've begun to regret this second sweater. Tonight seems warm for January.

A: Maybe you've just generated heat ascending through The Ramble.

J: Right, if I go two days without generating heat on a walk I'll lose it. I grow weak, tired, lethargic—you can say anything except… yeah I turn weak and tired. Daily life becomes difficult to execute. I'll feel…

A: Enervated? Listless?

J: myself fall away from the world.

A: I've never understood the word winsome but…

J: Winsome. I used to know. I memorized two-thousand words for the G.R.E. Do you like how backs of benches catch a glow from streetlamps?

A: I do.

J: And I love with wire fences, how separate strands glow from time to time. This past summer, hiking a mountain in Santa Fe, I'd watch sun gleam along strands of a spider's web.

A: Hmm I wanted to say: I'll appreciate when lamps and damp branches cause a spider-web…

J: Ooh.

A: effect.

J: Yes and physicists from previous generations lived so closely attuned to visible nature that they noticed this property of light and…

A: They didn't sleep in dark M.I.T. basements.

J: A windowless basement, where such phenomena don't get observed.

A: With rainforest screen-savers bouncing across the the...

J: Aristotle's *Nicomachean Ethics* addresses this poverty of ethical language. Aristotle says (he's talking about Ancient Greek of course), he'd he'll try to map the means and extremes of various qualities, like courage. Somebody too courageous we'd call— what negative extreme would you...

A: Foolhardy.

J: Foolhardy. And then somebody lacking courage altogether our...

A: Cowardly.

J: A coward, right. But he finds examples where you can't note extremes. Language does not provide ethical vocabulary for...

A: You mean this about ethics alone? Think of Wittgenstein's *Remarks on Colors*. His idea color gets defined through difference, through what it is not: that...

J: Doesn't...

A: we can't describe blue's essence other than...

J: The opposite...

A: of orange, perhaps?

J: That's what he says, since color vocabulary determines which colors we see; how, because we have three primary colors in our game, it's inconceivable for there to be a fourth or fifth. So he thinks about our incapacity to understand essence, but also our incapacity to look through broader frames since each…since language-games form the eyeglasses through which we see things. And if if you recall, we got onto this topic following that delicate perception you'd offered two mintues ago—light shining through an, through a, wet branches, creating the illusion of a spider's web. Imagine if in grade school we'd learned that…

A: Sure.

J: Yet the phenomenon doesn't exist for most people.

A: If you've, have you looked at, let's say Bruce Chatwin's book on indigenous Patagonians? How…

J: No.

A: many distinct terms exist for types of friendship, for example?

J: Is that right?

A: Or ennui: defined as "the absence of male friends."

J: Well thankfully I don't suffer from…

A: From what this is called?

J: Precisely. Because because of my...

A: Here we stand atop Belvedere Castle. How thrilling to reach the edge.

J: It is.

A: Again so many scenes in this park correspond to Hiroshige's *Hundred Famous Views of Edo*. At some point I hope, if no one has, to rediscover those the Edo sites. Most got paved. Pedestrians ought to...

J: During Japan's rise...

A: Or one became a nasty canal...

J: Really?

A: no one walks near anymore. Just as Canal Street started off a canal in...

J: I didn't know...

A: New York.

J: I'd never put that together.

A: Sorry to interrupt.

J: No you'd, you, it's funny; you can't see ducks and geese, yet we'll see...

A: [*Muffled*] trace?

J: the legs of the V—right, we can see their wakes. Those those ever-expanding legs of a V...

A: Beyond...

J: at which lone birds remain the point.

A: [*Muffled*] where it begins. Like exhaust dissipating from a jet, this...

J: Yes.

A: threshold from steel to sky...

J: That forms...

A: very clear and moving swiftly southeast from here.

J: It's a good, it's a great exercise in deduction, and if I ever lead a logic class I'll bring my students to bodies of water at night. If if if if, um, if if if...I picture the argument as follows: If if ducks swim in the pond, then you'll see the wake I just described. You see the wake I described. Therefore hidden...

A: Right. [*Pause*] It doesn't make sense. Is that right?

J: No it does.

A: Could you start again?

J: If if, ok…if we see the the wake I've just described…

A: Oh, if there's…

J: I'm sorry. Yes. I missed an, I…

A: Got it.

J: missed…

A: Remember who…

J: I put our…

A: took the L.S.A.T. recently.

J: Right.

A: Which forced me to refute your your case. This would have been a…what would it have been? Insufficient cause? Does…

J: Yes, since…

A: Just because sometimes you'd find, there's wake from ducks, wake doesn't mean…

J: Thank you. Thanks for correcting me. This second sweater's much too warm and—we'd talked about minute adjustments with clothes, or fans, which could be pointed…

A: Did you hear that honker with with…

J: Yeah I wonder if we caught that on tape.

A: wings squeaking past? [*Silence*]

J: But I can't make a minute adjustment now, so my brain's shut…

A: My fingertips feel like mossy stones. Maybe we should keep walking.

LATE SPRING

People about to collapse (emotionally) must often stand beneath.

MONDAY

I didn't put contacts in because of blotchy corneas. The blossoms beyond my glasses resembled distant snowcapped mountains. From the example of a bald man squatting under a bus-stop sign I projected everyone embracing today with a casualness I lacked. So I turned around amid the acoustical preface to "Hotel California." My apartment felt like refuge from a punishing sun. I put in my contacts and, with one eye pulsing, passed from Don Henley's voice to 8:37 brightness. Luis glanced up from his tools. He ignored my nod. Heavy traffic held me at the curb just long enough to generate penned-in hysteria.

In the park a woman kept saying "turtle" as she spoke of bygone springs spent with a brother. I wondered what response she so craved from her boyfriend. Crabapple boughs (a guess) bloomed out from the general green. The Meer lay glassy. My neighbor with a wheelchair and beret passed slowly—so his dog could piss before the leash went taut. A Korean girl smiled to confirm the sad respect we shared for this elder. A redwing blackbird spun displaying its stripes. A heron poking along the water's edge slalomed through reeds whenever possible.

Out of shoulder-deep muck stepped a normal pigeon; it climbed ashore and shook off. A woman performing knee bends looked confused. Approaching obnoxious boys I blanked. Willows had dropped fuzzy wormy strands. An old ashen beech twinkled.

Inside the Gardens a squirrel broke a branch and sniffed. The Untermeyer Fountain stood flowing again. A young gay white guy in heavy-framed glasses led five tough teens around the blandest tulips. A student whispered That's the lady from the office. Where she pointed a woman did tricep-building push-ups. Benches bearing Freshly Painted signs resembled dark horses with glossy coats. Mist among magnolias inspired me to pass through gardeners' sprays. As

I turned in I found figures wearing facemasks and full bodysuits. Orange lamplight glowed under thickening branches.

I exited surrounded by wiry women with powder-blue sweat-shirts that said Volunteer. Late-blooming narcissi pleased me most: Pixit, Jenny, Lemondrops. Jewel of Spring tulips contained all I'd ever wanted (like Morning Glory muffins). Those Virginia Bluebells, someone said, will be gone before you know. The trucks roaring down Fifth sounded like a fantasy. The lilacs explained my itchy pupils.

A pony-tailed photographer said Hi from where he lay on slabs, sounded kind and real—made the sixties seem a country people still could visit from. Police vans made the trail I climbed a squeeze. Near the compost heap one shady mound turned into a man awakening with stubble. Birders exchanged binoculars, consistently dressed in long dark coats. From Rustic Bridge #32 I watched a Raisinettes box glisten. The pulled weeds looked like watercress.

The waterfall just past Huddlestone Arch deserves sustained attention. People about to collapse (emotionally) must often stand beneath. Sunbeams rippled against thick stalks. I wanted to compliment the broken glass. A bicyclist hit stairs, veered towards dirt, partially spinning onto Park Drive traffic. The lingering puddles in Lasker Rink would dry this afternoon.

A turtle stretched its neck farther than I thought possible. I told a swan There's watery light reflecting off your belly. One smiling black man propped his head on the thinnest of papers (AM News). One Asian man did bizarre torso twists and two white girls mimicked his routine.

Amid fluorescent light in Parkview Deli I sensed how much other mornings differed from mine. As a carpenter strained to recall coworkers' requests the sandwich-girl's thigh pulsed. A deliveryman spun about desperate for somebody to sign his invoice. A Mexican boy in a cowboy hat made hauling a guitar seem easy. An African woman strode south with blue laundry bags on her head. My left eye had pinked slightly. My right one held a dead bug.

TUESDAY

Klever (the ex-doorman) stood back behind the desk for a day, so I stopped and we discussed his kids. I didn't check my cellphone on the way out because I didn't want Klever to think I hadn't enjoyed our talk. But when I got to Church it was 12:21. Leaving at lunch hour left me dizzy. My grandpa's blue raincoat sealed most pores. I sensed why painted bodies die. I noticed the distinct shape of every building. It felt like flickers of consciousness around my family.

By Reade I'd turned woozy—passing a Bento Box cart covered in Grand Opening signs, then caught between a rottweiler and an aggressive cocker spaniel. Someone screamed at the spaniel's owner Move! Walk away! I'm trying, the woman said, I don't know what's *happening*!

The situation dissolved except lingering stares. A boy appeared in ersatz medieval armor, tapped his sword every second step. A tired woman glared back like I'd checked her out (but I only started looking once she checked out me). Plum branches bloomed along a parking garage.

Still adjusting to humidity I almost caused a crash at the complicated Park Row intersection. A Fung Wah bus driver stood stiff wearing sunglasses. An old Asian man seemed to sense how stylish his brown bell-bottoms were. Across the street both stores sold bulletproof vests; I can't believe cops aren't given that stuff.

I cut towards the McDonald's off Bowery, desperate for a bathroom, pessimistic about my chances. Maudlin flute music played inside. Bland woodblock prints and ferns surrounded a two-floor fountain. Appraising angular lamps on my push upstairs I wondered if the Asian theme targeted tourists or locals. I was the only white person in the place. I would have told a line of girls the men's room sat empty but didn't know if this might come across as insulting. I left feeling soothed.

Mott Street's charming vertical signs mitigated my return to weird air-pressure. I swerved onto Aldrich past a long austere post office. A stylist dried salon windows with just an index card. A bike lay curled and melted. I could hear my heart beat for about a block. Then I was back on Bowery: watching pairs of women sift through rhinestones.

As always when I'm in a rush downtown I passed a sandwich shop that looked appealing. With a pulley-system someone dropped planks through an apartment window (no sound). With a tiny broom a custodian steered hissing water along the curb. Somebody else wrapped a deli display-case in blue plastic. Someone wiped the demonstration slicer he had whirring on the sidewalk. I wondered why everything in restaurant-supply stores looks dusty. A white truck double-turning (does that make sense?) stripped the fender off an old black woman's sedan. Pedestrians winced.

Potted geraniums along the Bowery Bar wall left me worried rowdy people would push them over. Pint glasses glared from a stoplight box. The cab of a UPS truck looked breezy. A rotund man walked like each step was a cringe. Rosary beads? he mumbled. I sensed but somehow never saw necklaces on a hanger. I stopped to watch kids play soccer with a green fuzzy size-4 ball. I wondered why workers' gloves often have the palm dyed dripping red. What had seemed a taxi flashed sirens—made everyone pull to the curb.

As we approached Union Square perfume off one white woman's fringe left me feeling passive. In James Madison Park teens slept sitting with dark cloth tied around their face. Behind them various newspapers had been hung to dry. Behind this stood a pine oak from James Madison's yard. Close to it a boy bit into something pink.

Somebody stared down a cab about to cut him off and I smiled because I'm often that person. Somebody sticking his head from a van tucked it back in like I'd wanted to kiss him. When I dropped a quarter one man leapt as if to prove he wasn't stealing. Standing straight I almost collided with a couple. Amid a jostling crowd as the walk sign changed I couldn't really see.

WEDNESDAY

Pale mist at 9:03 felt like my natural weather. I wondered if my hair looks best foggy mornings. I glanced back and saw Frankie wearing goggles. Hello, he called, instead of his usual OK!

Honking geese made the morning lucid and tender. Dandelions hadn't been there Tuesday. A West African curling dumbbells spoke to his daughter in the prettiest French. A jogger in a coolie hat barely moved forwards. I turned into the North Woods just as three gay Germans (two shaved bald) stepped out. An hour later I'd see them in the East 100s.

As I ascended towards greenness two white-bellied birds I'd thought were blue jays sang. Though Thoreau stresses being still in the woods I couldn't sit and wait for rustlings to reveal their sources. After more bad job news and predawn insomnia I wanted to know this world with me walking through it. A man with dreads drinking coffee and I kept weaving past each other on divergent trails. A worker stood on woodchips placing calls. I crossed two bridges that don't get named in the 150th Anniversary Map and Guide but iron grids directing The Loch somehow spoke to all that history.

Climbing loose rock into North Meadow I came out on three kids and a baseball diamond. The two boys sat silent in orange sweatshirts with numbers. The blonde girl in glasses giggled looking up. A guy bounced near handball courts waiting for a game.

I passed two mutts really going at it: the owners talking politely as if someplace else. The top dog got pulled when a Parks Enforcement vehicle approached. Two officers stepped out. The bottom-dog's owner apologized for removing its leash. I'm sorry, she said, I just thought with all this space. I'm sorry, I kept hearing, but I could only see the police truck. I'm sorry I'm sorry.

The East Meadow lay almost absent of dogs. I couldn't tolerate one airedale's master's strides. Planners assembling a stage at the Park's edge stood split along a giant extension cord. From the Fifth Ave. wall someone watched with a frown. It was obvious he wanted work.

The billowing outfit of the woman stepping from a bus somehow never obscured her pleasant shape. Our paths met at the Arthur Brisbane memorial. Brisbane sounded familiar, but the overwrought catalogue of his achievements suggested a gulf between now and 1936. A doorman and a poodle jogged past with both appearing to do it for the other's health.

In The Gardens plaid-skirted girls with Spencer sweatshirts sat on tiles sketching Texel Blues. Queen of the Nights and Esthers looked promising (though my walks are never timed right for tulips). The Actaea narcissus finally showed itself lovely. New staff taking notes followed a barrel-chested trainer. More Star Magnolias, she said. You saw a lot of them in Queens.

Beyond the gates Hispanic boys rode bikes and gnawed at Good Humor ice cream, mostly King Cones. A furtive Peruvian adjusted his fishing rod. Across The Meer I saw Luis—or someone of similar proportions and in the same ribbed shirt—stretch his calves. I'd never thought of Luis as a jogger.

Exhausted ladies laughed outside La Hermosa. They didn't seem all that religious but had definitely entered a protective space. A double-decker bus cruised past labeled North Loop: Harlem/Museum Mile/Park. A futon frame slipped from a garbage man's shoulder. I've always found garbage-truck rhythm soothing. Trophies propped a window on W. 112th. One showed a football player get tackled. Another vertically spelled out SCIENCE. In the next room a rustic frog-troupe played banjos; this I think was Senegalese.

In Family Horizons cups stood marked with kids' names and bean types. Ribbons flapped in front of Martin Luther King Jr. Senior Citizens' Center. On the next block a baseball diamond lay overrun with weeds. A bumper sticker read Born with nothing... and I've still got it! A senior-citizen van decomposed. A woman waited with crossed arms while a bus scooped her wheelchair.

THURSDAY

At 9:00 Kristin's front hall smelled like lilies. A woman wrapped a silk scarf around her ears. A reedy Asian girl followed her dad, stroking her scooter forwards. Crossing Church I sensed this one skyline image gradually replacing most childhood memories.

Wine we'd drunk to celebrate Kristin staying in New York left me scattered. Delivery-cart tracks rolled in and out of puddles. At the end somebody stacked soda cases. City Hall reflected in the deep blue part of windshields. Giant light bulbs had duct-tape at their tops. A driver slept with his mouth agape, looking like a Francis Bacon. A twelve year-old with an earring tilted his head and stared.

A Canadian trucker's gap-toothed smile reminded me I'd dreamt of kissing pink cotton. I remembered another dream (hiding long fingernails; then a cavernous house my mom had rented, with pink confetti in the front bushes).

On E. Broadway a monk wearing saffron robes peered out from his storefront temple. He seemed impatient. Several nearby institutions had titles approximating World Center for Buddhist Thought.

Somebody androgynous with feet propped on garbage bags cooed. Someone's boss watched storefront gates rise. In the Wing Yung Public School window kids' names hung posted to sheep and swans. Generators lit a fruit-market's lamps. I passed the Confucius statue considering the other statue—in Chatham Square, dedicated to the first anti-drug advocate in China—puzzled by this entire history, presuming we'd forced opium on a lot of people.

Climbing the Manhattan Bridge I saw carts canted toward the curb. Behind a power box two bodies lay zipped in rainbow sleeping bags. A pink cherry below on Bayard lost none of its charm beside ugly municipal buildings. Division remained the most "real" street I'd ever seen in New York—what was it, the dimensions? How a figure's always cutting diagonally across?

The closest roof prompted further questions: Do taggers just lean and paint downwards? I felt like I'd read a lot lately about the specific political roots of graffiti. Where I stepped somebody had written RACECAR. The next patch said Consider: 4% of Chinese are registered to vote. A sleek silver D-train ascended.

Laundry hanging in sixth-floor kitchens could have signified economic ingenuity or despair. I passed my ex-girlfriend Abby's building trying to guess which room was hers. A Q-train shot by next to me. Fences on both sides shuddered. I kept withdrawing, away from the cold, petrifying like some disappointed reptile. Water-taxis took forever to disappear. Waves blowing northeast spiraled sometimes. As spray crashed over Pearl Street's rocks someone who looked like me took photographs. Cobblestones turned vivid when somebody crossed. Dumbo's office-lofts stood solid.

Fences corralled me to Sands and Jay. Brooklyn felt even colder than the bridge. I grew frustrated behind construction vehicles. I got lost in an endless courtyard filled with crown-like tulips resembling Westpoints. Further up Tillary I found a Brooklyn Bridge entrance. One boy passed with cornrows: driving jauntily but clutching a tissue wad. A well-scrubbed cop eyed my hood skeptically. A strip of dry leaves swirled like a dragon.

The Jehovah's Witness clock's flashing spaced me out. Staten Island seemed hilly and half-covered in shade. I wanted to ask one woman if she needed help (though economically she looked fine). The song "Candy" by the band Cameo emerged from my past to overwhelm most of this bridge crossing. Everyone spoke Italian and paused erratically. My ears clogged to the point where two congestions touched.

Along Park I read about the Senate leader's fiery speech to some church of 10,000. "We Got the Beat" drifted from an adjacent bar. On my walk back to the elevators Raphael ducked behind his desk (delighting some kids). On the ride up I considered how nothing irritates me more than getting arrested by an infant's gaze. I'd taken my pants off before the door had closed, needing my legs to rub gentle air. I had to run warm water on my hands before I could write anything.

FRIDAY

None of the clothes I'd washed in the sink had dried. I had to put back on what I'd worn before showering. Someone trailed me on the way downstairs. She hurried past the mailboxes. It turned out she had a bus to catch and she sprinted in front of it, the way I will, holding it in place. I nodded at where Luis squatted beside a wheelbarrow.

Along The Meer a girl flinched each time she brought her cigarette close. When I passed the playground I was thinking whoever fired my brother must be a total prick, hoping my mom felt no whiplash after getting rear-ended last night, wondering if I've strayed too far from grounded pessimism or if I'm just less afraid of failure.

My trail sank beneath the 110th Street Bridge. I'd wanted to continue west but felt reluctant to turn while a foppish black man and German shepherd approached. This stranger's Good morning was classy and kind. One stray daffodil got me thinking Shouldn't I love this? Isn't this what I am? But it grew boring to be so metaphoric.

Along 108th I understood why businesses include that street in their titles. It seemed the perfect distance from more crowded blocks. A woman sprayed blue mist and wiped gunk from her dashboard. From one rearview mirror dangled mini Puerto Rican boxing gloves. From the next hung a Native American hoop. On the Southern Baptist church—with its name set perpendicular to form a cross at the T's—a taped-up sign just read Cuidado. Two girls sat in the front of a red sedan reading thick books, using bookmarks.

I passed pastry shops I would have tried by now if the neighborhood didn't get so sketchy at night. Watching deliverymen I wondered why people spit. Where I turned into Riverside Park someone who looked just like my friend Mike Yusko sat smoking, grinning—just as Mike would if he got up this early. I glanced his way assuming he'd acknowledge me first, since it's easy to recognize somebody walking. Below us the city had recently installed a triceratops and tyrannosaurus you could climb. Pink cherry blossoms lined the promenade (I knew I'd never pass under them).

A townhouse I otherwise appreciated held patriotic ribbons wrapped around the porch. A dog crossed with its owner calling Stephen, wait! Two Scottish terriers looked less intelligent side-by-side. An old Japanese woman wore a bowler hat. The question Was she attractive? made no sense. I was attracted to her. She needed my gaze and I delivered it.

Around New Moon Bakery it became clear that my gay side went for guys losing hair color, sporting metallic tones, with refined but somewhat stodgy taste in music. In front of a deli I learned one-hundred days of the new Bush presidency had passed. One cell-phone place also specialized in "sexy tongue rings" and, considering a photo from the movie *Thirteen*, I thought about how sexy they truly are, except when they make someone lisp, but even that's sometimes especially sexy. One bike-shop display presented women pulling at bikini bottoms. I couldn't tell if New York was a sensual city.

From under a cab poked a pizza box printed with dewy tomatoes. Tony Alamo Christian Ministries left imitation newspapers on select windshields. The headlines read Flood. My eyes followed one fire escape to a flock of Happy 5th Birthday balloons. I wondered if that's a big deal in Hispanic culture. As someone wearing a puffy jacket performed Tai Chi on her building's lawn I wondered how much of it was psychological. I felt like I move so much more than her while stretching.

Accelerating down 109th I fell in with a group approaching the B-C entrance. It appeared I was about to board a train. Concrete slabs twirled high above. A construction worker spoke casually with a friend while walking across a pit on a beam. Someone carrying a child chipped soccer balls over the playground fence. The defter he dribbled the more desperate it got.

Two cooks and one distracted woman made an intense triangle. How's six-thirty? the meek white guy said. *Please* let me think, the woman replied, now do you have a dollar?

On my own block I passed Slavs staring out from a truck platform, pointing and leering into the park. I kept waiting for them to say something so the moment could feel complete. Passing Frankie seemed so repetitive I didn't care how nice he was. I whined about our hallway reeking of incense. Sifting through stray envelopes I forgot what mail I wanted.

LATE WINTER

"...the smell of mice, stews, hip-cream and altitude, tenth-floor altitude."

UNION SQUARE W.F. (a natural grocery store), 8:30 p.m.

J: ...great returning to Union Square W.F.—the place where this whole project got conceived.

A: I especially like having a wall to our backs, a solid stomach filled by a well-balanced meal, and this rooibos tea. Thank you for it.

J: Do you like the rooibos?

A: I do; I associate its taste with color, a reddish color. Is the tea red...

J: Yes.

A: somehow? Or does the "roi" just make me think so? I'll sense a nice orangish, amberish, gleaming reddish hue on my tongue.

J: The tea's delicious. I'm happy to give it to you.

A: So where were you so long? While I waited?

J: Oh a man stood changing in the bathroom stall. Sorry it took so long. He entered wearing a biker's uniform and came out dressed for a waiter or host position.

A: Sure half my days I'll bring a change for the bathroom.

J: And you'll take your time changing as this man did? I imagine...

A: No, very rushed.

J: you'd rip through it.

A: I've once pulled muscles in my back getting a a foot stuck in pant-legs, thinking I'd taken them off when really I still sat entangled, yanking the waist and having my body follow.

J: Did you call in sick that day or or head to work?

A: I had just arrived. I packed the clothes and got down to...

J: Did you apply ice to your back?

A: No I didn't.

J: No.

A: I change clothes so much since I'll...we've said because we're Polish we sweat a tremendous amount. I'll worry I'm catching a cold from drafts I only feel because I've been perspiring.

J: Yeah, I've thought a lot about heritage lately. The other night somebody asked my heritage—a girl. Often that amounts to a pick-up line right, getting people to...

A: The first thing she'd...

J: talk about themselves? Shortly after introducing ourselves she asked my heritage.

A: It might suggest "I am aware of you as a body."

J: Hmm.

A: "I'm trying to assimilate these characteristics into an understanding of who you are deep down inside."

J: And she seemed shocked by my answer: Part Polish, part Chinese and part Haitian.

A: Right.

J: A look of perplexity crossed her face, so I felt I should explain myself. I said I'd got some Polishness and some, some Polish and Germanic blood from my parents, but that from two influential roommates I'd gained Chinese and Haitian characteristics. For example, if I hang jogging clothes all over the apartment to dry I feel distinctly Haitian.

A: Could that could that...

J: This is something Mrs. Merlin would do.

A: She'd of course...

J: My eighty-year-old roommate on the Upper West Side.

A: she of course wasn't jogging.

J: She wasn't jogging, though she would not pay to have clothes dried, and would hang clothes on hangers throughout the apartment.

A: I think I recall a busy apartment—with Mrs. Merlin applying cream to her hip in what looked like a crib to me.

J: Oh that's her brass day-bed. She did not sleep in a crib (yet she could appear as tiny as an infant). You saw the brass day-bed, which her nephew purchased at a store on 112th.

A: Or I remember several stews cooking simultaneously...

J: Yes.

A: many afternoons.

J: Friends from the building used our kitchen. I'd assume they had their own fully operational kitchens, but inevitably they'd come cook enormous bowls, pots of stew.

A: Goat? Goat?

J: Goat meat factored into many recipes.

A: They did this to spend time with Mrs. M. do you think?

J: I think so.

A: I've pictured some apparatus in a shower stall, or just outside.

J: She kept a medical chair in the bathtub. Every morning, after waking and stretching...though I didn't stretch first thing back then. Now I'd stretch first thing; but back then I stretched mid-afternoon.

A: It makes no sense.

J: It makes no sense, and if I had thought about it the slightest bit, if I had questioned that practice, I would've recognized its foolishness and revised it immediately. Yet it had gone unquestioned so long. Still anyway I would wake up, and the first thing I'd do, the first thing I'd touch, would be this hospital chair. I'd remove it from the bathtub...

A: Was it pink? I I...

J: It was pink, yes, as were the shower curtain...

A: Ok.

J: and floor-tiles, and the walls themselves stood painted pink.

A: I do remember...

J: [*Voices*] full pink bathroom.

A: a monochromatic sensation. Now I've...you couldn't put towels in the bathroom?

J: I'd left mine there the first week or so, but it acquired an awful smell.

A: From the room itself?

J: Well it made contact with Mrs. Merlin's towel, and ordinarily—I mean which shocked me, since she herself I thought smelled nice...

A: Oh see, I'd wanted to say, I also remember the smell of hip-cream permeating not just the living-room and kitchen areas, but your bedroom as well.

J: Yeah.

A: I'll remember the smell of…

J: The smell of dead mice too, do you remember that smell?

A: Yeah I was going to say: I remember the smell of mice, stews, hip-cream, smoke (cigarette smoke) and altitude, tenth-floor altitude.

J: Tenth floor. Most afternoons I'd [*Voices*] sun set over New Jersey. I'd sit reading Montaigne at my desk, smoking half-cigarettes, as was my style back then, and look out two windows toward pink sky.

A: I seem to recollect square pillows? Almost couch pillows?

J: Mrs. Merlin, like most women I've met, had an excess of pillows. And the room came furnished with a half-dozen square pillows. Some nights you stayed until four-thirty before catching the first bus back to Astoria, where you lived then, and we would use these pillows. I'd spread some a across the bed and you'd sleep off bits of the hangover.

A: I would wake with with contacts stuck flat to my eyeballs, in a way they never get from a full night's sleep, then exit with my organs shivering to catch an M-60 bus to Astoria. That fall I'd enter the bagel shop just as it opened—4:50 a.m.

J: Did the owners call you by name?

A: The man who opened this store didn't own it. He came from Central America and couldn't speak English, yet...

J: Were there any...

A: though still he recognized me.

J: So he showed signs of recognition?

A: Oh absolutely, and joy. He'd unlock both doors and face the the consequence cranky customers followed me in, but I was like the sun to that place.

J: And you'd enter a shop filled with warm bakery smells?

A: Yeah I'd watch conveyor-belts of bagels (somehow in water). They seemed to float like inner tubes. I don't know if you've seen a bagel operation like this.

J: I haven't. Would you sleep on the bus, or try to?

A: I could never sleep on busses or in a classroom for that matter.

J: Do you retain thoughts you'd have riding from my Upper West Side ghetto-apartment back to your...not exactly ghetto but...

A: I'd call it palatial...

J: It looked...

A: yet provincial at the same time.

J: Right.

A: A home for gentry. Um I didn't form thoughts. I'd—if you've had: you know waking early to catch an airplane, for example (riding through a still-darkened city...

J: Hmm.

A: feeling both more lucid and less lucid than you could...

J: And did...

A: with words). That feeling came often.

J: Though now you'd...

A: That fit perfectly riding on a bus.

J: still—yeah I wanted to ask if you felt fortunate to face circumstances...

A: Did I...

J: [*Voices*] have those feelings?

A: I'd sit so at peace with surroundings I forgot to feel fortunate.

J: Oh.

A: I felt simply in motion.

J: Ok.

A: At other points I probably seemed depressed. One night you and I danced in my kitchen (with me at least stripped to my underwear) to Prince. Prince cheered me up.

J: This all happened five years ago right?

A: Just after September 11th but...

J: Yes.

A: before I met my honey.

J: Then more recently than five years ago, more like four years ago.

A: We can get precise if necessary—since...

J: No you, I'm happy to say four/five years ago.

A: Sure.

J: Just so we don't give the impression that this took place ten...

A: Certainly not. We haven't known each other that long. [*Silence*] So I'm curious if today felt different [*Voices*] our fun night. I'll have few thoughts after fun nights, and this morning my concentration broke. My mind kept drifting to topics I'd discussed, to anticipations of future meetings with people we saw, recombinations of events and scenarios and rooms I stood in.

J: Right I've I turned down Thanksgiving invitations as a student. I'd use holidays to draft papers and assemble...

A: An important time.

J: thoughts. I agree. Others couldn't understand this behavior, but it made sense to me, and...

A: I'll remember...

J: I would remember certain passages. I'd call to mind quotes from Emerson that justified my moods. He himself would guard his mood, he says, since no one else can grasp what our moods require. Um I also didn't complete much work today. Amanda called with the, good news. She'll visit next weekend.

A: Exciting.

J: Yeah; which sounds exciting. She'll spend two full nights (Friday and Saturday) then ride back to Boston on a Sunday Fung Wah.

A: I'd...speaking of Thanksgiving: I remember in my second year of college, preparing by December to be done, to graduate. I'd taken the G.R.E. so began writing essays, entrance essays, for programs, you know graduate applications.

J: Really? I never knew you'd applied to graduate departments back then. For English literature?

A: For African-American literature, or history. I'd been a history major, or an Afro-American-history major.

J: Not to mention a consultant for high-ranking Senate...

A: Um, congresspeople. Still I was drafting one final seminar paper.

I'd developed a three-dimensional notecard system which took up most of the bedroom. Yet half halfway through organizing these discrete thoughts into coherent sequence I lost my place, suffered a slight nervous breakdown, got first consoled by my mother but then, then told it's socially inappropriate to turn pre-occupied and deranged.

J: During holidays? Or...

A: General...

J: in general?

A: [*Muffled*] all momentum, barely finished the paper, and decided twenty's too young for graduate school.

J: So I took a walk this afternoon after talking to Amanda—to relish our conversation and imagine spending...

A: Just bef...

J: new lovely moments together. As I stepped out I saw a Caribbean church service start. To my left stands the Celestial Church of Christ, in the Alare Alua Parish.

A: Do you find it hard to read whole church names?

J: Oh oh sure. That's difficult.

A: Celestial would have thrown me.

J: Yeah, I'd pulled out a pen...

A: I see.

J: and a paper scrap to assist my memory. I soon went back to my apartment but many hours later—I'd say five hours later—as I left for the A-train to come here to meet you I noticed the church service just letting out. The worshippers all wore silky white robes with...

A: Everybody?

J: headdresses: except the little kids.

A: Men and women both?

J: Wore the exact same gowns.

A: You'd you mentioned paths to the subway station. Lately I never stop moving walking up or down Manhattan. So long as you stay aware of what the the upcoming light says you can run and make it (though this gets hard [*Cough*] Holland Tunnel). But I'll wonder if you find New York walks continuous as they would be, say, on the hills of Santa Fe—or has there been jostling, pausing, restarting?

J: No I've shared your smooth continuous experience, and I haven't read much Lyn Hejinian, but she makes the same remark in *My Life*.

A: About New York specifically?

J: Yes about New, about how this great metropolis provides the sensation of crossing through sheer wildern...

A: Hmm.

J: And I've noticed…

A: That sounds slightly different.

J: even if my path gets blocked by cars or a Don't Walk sign, I can cut to side-streets since I'll have no destination.

A: I'll save side-streets as long as I can, so when I need one I'm ready to turn.

J: Sure I love in this city the constant dialogue between drivers and pedestrians. It also…

A: And, let's say, deliverymen…

J: Exactly.

A: street vendors…

J: What great…

A: and hangers-out, hangers-about on the street…

J: Yet another great…

A: men wheeling carts. Go ahead, yeah.

J: Yes you feel this great sense of cooperation.

A: Also of smoothness I find. I'd experience panic in a calmer city, early-evening hours when I'd just snap.

J: While I was running...when I walked back to my apartment today, a car, a a dri—as I walked back to the apartment today one driver made eye-contact with me, through her windshield, and allowed just enough time so I could cross an intersection before she passed through it. If I had hesitated (for example to tie my shoe) I'm sure we would have collided. She'd counted on the continuity of my my movement. I took part in mathematics of the most complex kind.

A: I do especially love that you...that in New York to hesitate means to cause others problems.

J: Yeah, since continuity remains the norm.

A: Now now do you think continuity can include fits of tension or violence, flare-ups, frustration? I for example, the other day, and I've been meaning to ask if—I gave a mom the finger...

J: But not...

A: in a station wagon: a mother and daughter. I didn't see the girl until too late. The mom kept trying to turn though clearly I had a Walk sign. She honked um at the presence of my body.

J: This happened in Tribeca?

A: Outside MoMA.

J: Ok.

A: So I flipped them off. Now could you...afterwards I, instead of feeling guilty, felt attuned to the momentary slip that...

J: Well...

A: But I don't know how she'd felt about it.

J: at first she might have felt insulted, but when she recalls the moment, if she does, I'm sure she considers your response appropriate. I remember crossing Broadway (around the mid-80s) as as a girl learning to drive turned an enormous SUV, nearly killing me, and we made eye-contact through the windshield, and so I started whacking off. I mean in an...I didn't pull my—I I didn't pull out my genitals; I'd simply, how should...

A: You gestured.

J: I gestured yeah, lewdly.

A: Though was this driver...

J: She seemed shocked.

A: accompanied? Did a driving coach accompany...

J: Yes, she and her mother stared with wide-open eyes.

A: Did they turn towards each other?

J: They looked much too frightened.

A: [*Voices*] glancing at my mom if, when swears came up in movies.

Go…

J: Then after making my lewd gesture I crouched.

A: Did your hips rock as well?

J: I got totally into it. I swayed my hips. Pedestrians behind me started laughing. They too almost had been crushed. A large SUV can take out groups…

A: Sure. The driv…

J: without difficulty.

A: the driver wasn't wearing sunglasses, was she? That would infuriate…

J: She wasn't wearing sunglasses. Nor was the mom. I saw their large eyes fixate on on my gesture. I then stopped gesturing, pointed and began to laugh loudly, and then I passed through the intersection and spanked my rear then pointed back at them—one final time, and kept walking. This all took four to five seconds.

A: Of fluid motion?

J: Precisely. But I hadn't left my apartment thinking Ah, the moment I encounter reckless drivers here's what I'll do. It came about naturally, and felt harmonious and continuous. I thank I thank the city for such episodes of maniacal grace.

A: I'd guess we both learned to drive in expansive department-store parking lots?

J: Yes.

A: Fools might consider that a luxury of space—not realizing it presumes a detachment from culture, and by culture I mean near-accidents.

J: Right I myself learned to drive in a public high-school's lot. I'd got trained on two stick-shifts, jolting…

A: I had my first oral-sex experience in a high-school parking lot, yet was not um the recipient. Um, this tea Jon, has started to develop a mace flavor? A bold spicy flavor? Will you often find that near the bottom of the cup?

J: It…

A: I've sensed a wooden quality, and spicy quality, circulating not only through my tongue and mouth but all down my chest. Thanks for that.

J: Yeah this this the tea seems meant, is is: the tea can make you feel kind of wild.

A: I could use some physical comfort, and I get that from the tea. I've had a problem with these shoes. When whenever I buy a pass, a seven-day or thirty-day subway pass, I'll dream the new pass won't expire. Do you have this thought? On the final day I'll think, Maybe [*Cough*] computer glitch and the pass can stay good forever. Do you, do…I've wondered if all New Yorkers share this thought.

J: On nights when a subway pass expires I'll try to remember which day I bought it. And I'll often grow confused calculating a week, thinking Maybe in the end I have an extra day since...well, if I buy the pass on Friday, it's good through the following Thursday; yet sometimes I fool myself into thinking it's good the following Friday.

A: I'll I don't want to abet your delusions, but occasionally I'm given that extra day.

J: Really?

A: Though I ask about subway passes because of a related fantasy when I buy sneakers. I'll think Maybe this new pair won't ever wear out. Now I seem to have found some New Balance (with light-blue stripes—perhaps you've seen them). I'd bought them sensing they look a little gay. We all should [*Voices*] gay sneakers.

J: But how...

A: However, those shoes have sat covered in mud since our walk through Central Park. The result...

J: Through Prospect Pa...

A: Central.

J: Oh.

A: And since then this old pair has destroyed my lower-back muscles. I purchased two meatballs for dinner tonight, and it feels like one lodged in each side of my back. How about you? What was your dinner?

J: Oh I ate some chicken. I've lived on tofu and broccoli out in Fort Greene from—such rude…

A: [*Muffled stretch*] sound ok?

J: Sure I'll stop it. [*Tape stops*]

***

J: So we abruptly stopped the tape.

A: I hope you don't mind moving.

J: Three guys, macho-looking guys with far too much testosterone sat sat at the adjacent table.

A: What is the testosterone-charged air is it, I haven't looked at them, is it their voices? Is it motions? I believe it's their motions that so bother me and (to New York's credit) bother everyone else.

J: Yeah and mock-turtleneck sweaters, with sunglasses on their head though it's dark outside.

A: You'd started to discuss your eating habits.

J: Well tonight, as I've hinted, I ripped off some chicken and baby tomatoes…

A: I'll love…

J: I'm fond of them too.

A: the instant before biting into one. When they'll roll in your mouth as you sense—what shape do they have?

J: They'd...

A: Not cylindrical, um, elliptical?

J: Or yeah...

A: Elliptical shapes?

J: like little eggs.

A: They make your tongue crack sensual.

J: Tonight I sprinkled twelve in my salad box, along with shredded carrots. I'd brought brown rice and an avocado-half from Brooklyn. I don't like eating grains here since as as we've said, they taste too salted. That leaves room in the box for more nutritious things.

A: Though grains fill the gaps like no other food.

J: True because...

A: There's always room for grains.

J: Just like um mortar...just like mortar pasting bricks...

A: Yes.

J: the grains have such small surface-volume they fit into gaps. But when I entered W.F.'s café I found you and Kristin eating dinner.

A: We'd, I walked to school and printed several books. Since we haven't taken advanta…

J: You got entire books? What books did you…

A: I printed a Hannah Weiner book, something about Indians. I printed up Rosemarie Waldrop's—oh I'm blanking on the name.

J: It doesn't matter.

A: Yeah as soon as something gets put on paper [*Cough*] chance I'll retain it. Or perhaps you know: when the Laotians began to write, which happened I believe mid-seventies (a French priest designed a print language for them), they lost half…

J: Socrates talks about this in the *Phaedrus*. He refuses to write since it would weaken his memory.

A: Hmm I've heard an implicit anxiety throughout Plato's work is that, for the first time ap appears the potential for discourse to be preserved—to pick up new interpretations the author couldn't anticipate, interpretation justified by textual proof. And this anxiety leads to conceptions, you know Platonic conceptions of forms (an idealized world; a world more permanent than the written one coming…

J: So you think Plato's disdain for the empirical world derives…

A: His…

J: [*Muffled*] books ambiguous?

A: Ambiguous in a way things hadn't been. A new temporality develops through them, as Plato's thought becomes our thought.

J: But fragments exist predating Plato. We have some Pythagoras, thanks to notes his disciples took.

A: Right, I don't know what made it more likely whole books would get preserved, that a text could be written rather than transcribed?

J: For…

A: I speak from five minutes in a botany class.

J: Still I I don't think Plato's the first person to make, to put thorough philosophical investigations on paper. Others before him composed treatises though I can't discuss that. I don't know the history. I don't, I don't know for example, I don't, I don't know how…when the Alexandria fire took place, but I know on account of it we lost tons of Aristotle, most of Diogenes and texts from…

A: Right. Right. Through that through…

J: pre-Socratics.

A: that fire?

J: Plato's writings somehow survived. Clean copies circulated.

A: Though did it help to have a large influential school? With students trying to learn from the master? Thinking if they assemble, perhaps horde his thought, they'd um, they'll become masters?

J: Well Diogenes describes young students flocking to Plato. Diogenes calls the Athenian youth just as "vain" as Plato himself. He uses that harsh term to characterize Plato.

A: Doesn't Diogenes remain harsh towards Plato overall? He's...

J: Oh yeah.

A: thrilled to keep an empty bowl before him, on the porches of Athens, rather than a a bounteous table in the palace of Syracuse or someone. He's scornful of Plato's ease around power.

J: And mistrusted Plato for possessing such wealth and, for what it's worth, Plato appears to scorn the body within his dialogues but—do you see our friend Stephen...

A: Wow.

J: Yosifon?

A: As we speak of Platonic forms in in one strides: a backpack off...

J: Yeah the Platonic form of a young man.

A: one shoulder, his lip curled under the teeth, a nod a nod from the Apollo right now. You'd mentioned talking to the Yos.

J: I tried to meet him for dinner while you sat with Kristin. Yet from—I should finish my point about Plato. He gave himself that name. It means "broad shoulders." Plato lifted weights in the agora, but Diogenes thought that a waste of time, because a true philosopher should walk around and eat barley cakes and not adopt extravagant physical habits. Of course I'd be reluc...

A: Doesn't Steve...

J: But yes, I've talked with Stephen, who stayed tight-lipped describing...

A: Physically, physically now, I do sense a tight-lippedness as...

J: He didn't want to discuss his date with José last night.

A: strong features cast a fierce shadow across his face; he looks like Matisse's...

J: Hmm.

A: "The Piano Lesson."

ACKNOWLEDGMENTS

The authors would like to thank Sandra Doller (*1913*) and Tim Peterson (*EOAGH*) for publishing excerpts from this book. They would especially like to thank Craig Dworkin for publishing Andy's *Sixty Morning Walks* project on Editions Eclipse.